ON THE BANKS OF THE FOYLE

To my mother and father, and Melody and Laura

The Friar's Bush Press
24 College Park Avenue
Belfast BT7 1LR
Published 1989
© Copyright reserved
ISBN 0946872 24 4

848   46593

Designed by Rodney Miller Associates, Belfast.
Printed by W. & G. Baird, Antrim.

On The Banks of the Foyle

Historic photographs of Victorian and Edwardian Derry

Brian Mitchell
of the Inner City Trust

FRIAR'S BUSH PRESS

Derry is a historic town. A small self-sufficient monastic community was established there in the 6th century A.D. Set around a small wooden church, the settlement was built in a clearing amongst the oak forest which clothed the island of Derry and gave it its name. There was a steady rise in the status and importance of Derry from 900 A.D. as it first succeeded Iona and then Kells as the centre of all Columban monastic foundations in Ireland and Scotland.

In the 12th century the monastic settlement of Doire Columkille was at the peak of its fortunes as the MacLoughlins, contenders for the High Kingship of Ireland, from their royal palace at Grianan of Aileach, bestowed their patronage upon it. In 1164 under the personal direction of Muireartach MacLoughlin, High King of Ireland, Templemore or "the great church" was built within a stone enclosure. Derry now had one of the biggest cathedrals in Ireland; worthy of her position as head of all Columban monasteries.

In the 13th century the new religious orders of continental Europe, the Augustinians, Cistercians and Dominicans, became established in Derry, only to fall into decline and finally to disappear in the 16th century. Today there are no physical remains of Derry's millennium as a monastic settlement. The link with this period is only retained in the place name, Long Tower, which refers to the round tower of stone, built sometime in the 11th century, which formerly stood there.

Owing to Derry's central position between the two powerful kingdoms of the O'Neills and the O'Donnells it became clear to English rulers attempting to pacify Ulster in the 16th century that Derry should be occupied, fortified and garrisoned. Sir Henry Docwra and an army of 4,000 succeeded in doing this in the year 1600.

A new dimension was added in 1609 with the Earl of Salisbury's suggestion to King James I of a plantation of English and Scottish colonists. James I approached the City of London to undertake the plantation of Derry and the County of Coleraine. A development corporation of the City of London, called The Irish Society, was set up to manage the plantation on 29 March 1613. By 1618 the city, now renamed Londonderry, was completely enclosed within a stone wall 24 feet high, and entered by four fortified gates, Shipquay, Ferryquay, Bishop's and Butcher Gates. The new town within the walls was of a functional grid pattern. From the four gates the four principal streets met in the open area or Diamond. All other streets then met the main streets at right angles. 92 houses extended along both sides of the four main streets, housing 102 families.

Between 1628 and 1633 a cathedral was built as a place of worship for the planters. The building material for much of the new settlement came from the buildings and ruins of the old monastic settlement. When Docwra arrived at Derry in 1600 the round tower of the monastery was still standing. Initially the old abbey, on the site of the present-day St Augustine's Church, was repaired, as a place of worship for the settlers until the construction of St Columb's Cathedral was completed in 1633. The walls, street pattern and cathedral of this plantation town survive to this day.

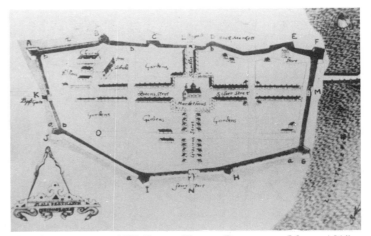

The plantation town, 1625. From a Thomas Raven map. (Magee A216)

In the 17th century Derry repulsed all attacks, hence her title, the Maiden City. She survived the famous Siege of Derry, relieved on the 105th day, the 12th August 1689 by the breaking of a boom which had been placed across the River Foyle. Derry's strategic significance was reflected in the fact that in 1700 it was the largest town in Ulster, with a population of some 2,000.

In the 18th century Derry began to experience a measure of economic growth which was quite marked from the 1770s. In the fifty year period to 1820, County Londonderry became one of the major linen producing areas in Ireland, and the city of Derry, one of its major markets. In 1770 a purpose-built Linen Hall was constructed on Rosemary Lane, later to be renamed Linenhall Street.

The importance of emigration established Derry as the chief Irish port for transatlantic trade in the 18th century. Trade with the West Indies and the 13 colonies of North America grew to such an extent that by the 1770s it rivalled even her coasting trade with Britain. In 1771, for example, the American colonies imported more linen cloth and food provisions from Derry than Britain did. Derry and Belfast established themselves as the main port of exit for the large scale emigration of Presbyterians from Ulster in the 18th century. It is estimated that 6,300 emigrants were carried on 22 ships which sailed from Derry for North America during the slump in the linen industry in 1771 and 1772.

In the fifty years from 1770 the volume and variety of Derry's trade with Britain increased very significantly. 1791 was the first year that over one million yards of linen cloth were exported through the port, and by 1821 four million yards were being shipped to Britain annually. Derry, furthermore, started to participate with some success in the provisions trade with Britain. Beef, butter, pork, ham and bacon exports all rose steeply.

By 1821, under the twin stimuli of a prosperous linen industry and of a growing port with extensive trade connections, Derry had become a growing, vigorous town of 9,313 souls. The two major commercial streets, Bishop Street and Shipquay Street, were busy and distinguished thoroughfares, with many service and craft industries. Engravings from the early 19th century illustrate this well.

On Bishop Street alone there were 56 businesses, some extending outside the city walls, including the linen warehouse of Thomas Mulholland & Co.; the bakery and distillery of Andrew Watt & Co., later to become the producer of the world-famous Tyrconnell whiskey, from premises in Abbey Street; and the premises of John Munn, agent for a shipping company, but later to become a ship owner and flax mill owner. These businesses existed side by side with small retailers, such as grocers, haberdashers, hatters, ironmongers and publicans and with small industries, such as boot and shoe makers, cabinet makers, rope makers, tanners and tobacco manufacturers.

Shipquay Street was very distinctive with a succession of typical Georgian houses, stepping up the hill; graceful, red brick buildings of three or four storeys, with entrances, owing to the street's steepness, by way of steps and balconies bounded with metal railings. There were some 20 businesses located here, and beyond the gate at Shipquay there were a further 21. The major merchants of Derry had their premises here, because the cargoes of timber, tea, sugar and many other items were landed at Shipquay. The masts of the sailing ships could be seen from the commercial areas of the town. To service the needs of the ships that used the port there were at Shipquay, hotels, blockmakers, coopers, rope makers, ship's brokers and ship's chandlers.

Throughout the 19th century Derry continued to thrive as an emigration port. Merchants in Derry now became ship owners, as opposed to agents for American and British Companies. In 1812 there was not one single Derry-owned vessel in the North American trade, but by 1833 there were 15, owned by seven merchants. The largest fleet of five ships belonged to John Kelso.

In the 1860s William McCorkell & Co. had a fleet of five ships plying between Derry, and New York and Philadelphia. One of these ships was the *Mohongo*. Built in 1851 by Samuel Smith of Oromucto, New Brunswick, Canada, the *Mohongo*, painted with white ports on a black hull and bearing an Indian squaw figurehead, served for twenty years in the passenger service to Philadelphia and Quebec. Her passenger voyages were normally 5 weeks out and 4 weeks home with the prevailing westerly winds behind her. She was sold in 1872, having made one hundred crossings of the North Atlantic under six different masters.

By the 1850s the passenger trade was dominated by the two firms, J. & J. Cooke and William McCorkell & Co. In the period 1847 to 1867 J. & J. Cooke carried 21,000 passengers to North America, of which well over 90% came from either Counties Londonderry, Donegal, Fermanagh or Tyrone. In this period the company bought nine ships specifically for the emigration trade.

From the 1870s steam took over from sail on the transatlantic routes. Right down to 1939, would-be emigrants were carried down the Foyle in paddle tenders from Queen's quay to connect with the steamships of the Anchor and Allan Lines that anchored, 18 miles downstream, at Moville.

In the ninety year period to 1911 the population of Derry quadrupled to 40,780. In 1821 Derry was the 12th largest town in Ireland, by 1911 she was the 4th. In 1821 Derry was only twice as big as her rivals, Strabane and Coleraine and four times the size of Letterkenny. By 1911 she was five times as big as Coleraine, eight times the size of Strabane and eighteen times the size of Letterkenny. During this period Derry stamped her dominance over her local rivals and emerged as an important urban centre within Ireland. The reason for this growth lies in the developments of the industrial revolution.

From the 1830s a succession of entrepreneurs appeared on the scene and established new industries or expanded old ones. In the space of fifty years the shirt industry grew from virtually nothing to become the principal seat of the shirt industry in the United Kingdom and exported all over the world. A local man, William Scott, laid the foundations for this new industry. In the 1850s Scott's initial success attracted a number of Scottish businessmen who brought with them the new methods of factory organisation and new technology in the form of the sewing machine. In 1857 William Tillie from Glasgow, together with his partner John Henderson, erected a five storey factory on Foyle Road, then the largest shirt factory in the world. Confidence in the shirt industry was reflected in the massive red bricked factories which were built at that time. Peter McIntyre from Paisley and Adam Hogg from Melrose opened the City Factory on Queen Street in 1864. The shirt industry provided predominantly female employment. In the 1870s the girls in Derry's shirt factories worked 51 hours per week, from 8 a.m. to 8 p.m. with one hour for lunch, for wages of 5 to 12 shillings per week. By 1900 the assembly line approach to shirt making dominated, with each worker specialising in a particular aspect of production. A shirt was now produced every two minutes, with each shirt passing through the hands of eight workers. By 1926 there were 44 shirt factories in Derry, employing 8,000 people and 10,000 outworkers.

The beginnings of shipbuilding can be assigned to Captain William Coppin who bought the yard and slip dock, belonging to Pitt Skipton and John Henderson, on the Strand Road in 1839. By 1840 he was employing 500 men in building new vessels, ship repairs and salvage work. Coppin's yard closed in 1870.

In 1882 shipbuilding returned to Derry when local man Charles Bigger set up the Foyle Shipyard at a new site at Pennyburn. This yard specialised in the construction of large steel hulled sailing ships. The yard built five such ships for local merchant, William Mitchell's, Foyle Line. The ships of the Foyle Line, such as the 2,035 ton *William Mitchell*, were seldom seen in the home port as they plied the great world trading routes. Sailing to Australia and then across the Pacific to the west coast of South America, with coal, and returning around Cape Horn, with nitrate, were the last remaining trade routes profitable for sailing ships. The yard closed in 1892, having built 7 steamships and 26 sailing vessels.

In 1899 with capital raised locally, the Londonderry Shipbuilding and Engineering Company Limited reopened the yard, but it was closed by 1904.

In 1912 Swan and Hunter, the Tyne shipbuilders took over the yard and set up the North of Ireland Shipbuilding Company. Four new berths were constructed. The yard now had the capacity to build ships of 9,000 tons. Within one year of setting up, the yard's future looked bright, as they secured orders for ten passenger and cargo steamers from a French company and a further eight steamers from a Canadian firm. During the First World War the yard was working 24 hours a day to replace allied shipping losses. By 1918 the workforce totalled 2,000 men. The workforce grew to 2,600 in the early 1920s, only to close in 1924 owing to the deepening world depression.

By 1830 Derry had a small whiskey distilling industry with distilleries at Pennyburn, Waterside and Abbey Street producing over 200,000 gallons of whiskey annually between them. In 1839 David Watt acquired full ownership of the Abbey Street distillery and began the expansion that was to make Watt's distillery one of the biggest in the United Kingdom. In 1870 David Watt took over the Waterside distillery. By 1887 the two Coffey patent stills, seven storeys high, within the eight acre Abbey Street complex, produced 1,260,000 gallons of grain whiskey annually. On the premises were five bonded stores, containing at any one time 30,000 casks of whiskey. This distillery was worked by a 230 horse power engine, one of the largest in any distillery in Ireland, and it employed 200 men. Its two chimney stacks of 130 feet and 160 feet acted as landmarks for shipping in the Foyle. At Watt's Waterside distillery 200,000 gallons of malt whiskey were produced annually. Like shipbuilding, the end for Watt's and its "Old Tyrconnel" grain whiskey and "Old Inishowen" malt whiskey, came with the depression and the resultant contracting markets of the 1920s.

Industrial growth was not just confined to the major employers of shirt making, shipbuilding and distilling. At the turn of the 20th century the Wellington Foundry of George Green & Co. and the Foyle Iron and Brass Foundry of A. Brown & Sons, each employed 100 men, making various types of machinery. Hugh Stevenson & Co., employed 90, in making bread and biscuits at William Street while John Brewster operated his model bakery at James Street. In Clarendon Street, James Young was the biggest carriage builder in the north of Ireland, with a showroom that displayed some 200 carriages. On Bishop Street, David Campbell and his workforce of 60 were the leading furniture manufacturers in the north west.

Derry's industrial strength and her extensive trading connections were complemented by a communications network which confirmed and reinforced the city's position, at the turn of the

Bishop Street in the 1830s. Photograph of a contemporary engraving. (Ulster Museum, Welch W07/17/28)

century, as the regional wholesale and retail centre of the north west of Ireland.

By 1910 Derry was the terminus of four railway lines. The Northern Counties Railway, from its station at the Waterside, ran the line to Belfast via Coleraine. The Great Northern Railway Company connected Derry to both Belfast and Dublin via Strabane and Omagh, from its terminus on Foyle Road by Carlisle Bridge. From its Strand Road station the Londonderry and Lough Swilly Railway Company owned or worked 100 miles of rail, mostly in north Donegal. In 1906 the County Donegal Joint Company was formed. It worked 124 miles of rail from the station at Victoria Road in the Waterside. This line essentially served south Donegal via Strabane. From 1867 to 1926 the Londonderry Port and Harbour Commissioners ran six miles of railway sidings on both sides of the Foyle, which were connected by track on the lower deck of Carlisle Bridge. This track was used solely to move freight along the quay to the four rail termini. With this rail network Derry was able to draw the produce of Counties Londonderry, Donegal, Fermanagh and Tyrone to its markets and quays.

Derry's business community was quick to grasp the importance of steam in developing the city's coasting trade with Britain. In 1829 the first steamer belonging to the port, the 136 ton paddle steamer *Foyle* was purchased for the Glasgow route. By 1836 the Londonderry and Glasgow Steamboat Company operated three boats on the Glasgow route, with the passage taking between 18 and 20 hours. At the same time the North West of Ireland Union Steam Company ran two boats on the Liverpool route, in a passage time of 21 to 23 hours. Up to the 1860s these companies remained in the control of Derry merchants. By 1868, however, the Glasgow firms of Alexander Laird and the Burns Steamship Company had eliminated the local operators on the Derry-Glasgow route while in 1866 the Belfast Steamship Company took over the running of the Liverpool route.

By 1901 Derry was served, every week, by two sailings to Glasgow on Burns' steamers, four sailings to Glasgow on Laird's steamers, two sailings to Liverpool by the Belfast Steamship Company and two sailings to Morecambe and one to Fleetwood on Laird's ships.

Always bear in mind when looking at the photographs in this book that they were taken at the height of Derry's development. In the thirty years to 1911 the population of the city doubled. Derry was then a place of opportunity, offering good employment prospects. Families from outside the city and county of Londonderry were

drawn there. In 1901, for example, of 31 households on Argyle Terrace nineteen had origins outside the county, ten of the heads of household were born in Scotland while eight had come from County Donegal. The shipyard and bakery were the major employers, with six of the heads of household working in the former and five in the latter. Not only did the head of the family find employment in Derry but so too did the rest of the family. In one family group on Argyle Terrace the father, born in Scotland, worked as a baker, while the 25 year old daughter found employment as an examiner in a shirt factory, the 18 year old son served as an apprentice baker and the 16 year old son worked as a rivet boy in the shipyard. The photographs in the book will give some idea of the vitality and architectural grandeur of Derry during this boom period.

These photographs are drawn from a number of sources. Much valuable material came from the major collections held at the University of Ulster, Magee College, the National Library in Dublin, the Ulster Museum, and the Ulster Folk and Transport Museums. The collections of helpful private individuals and local institutions, including the Derry City Council, were also used. The photographic sources contain vital information for us today, but they do have some limitations. They are restricted by the preoccupations of their time and the technical shortcomings of early photography. Nevertheless, the pages reveal much about a proud city at the height of its powers.

The McCorkell ship *Mohongo*, from a painting. (Magee C992)

CONTENTS

ACKNOWLEDGEMENTS

Many thanks are due to all those who shared in our enthusiasm in locating old photographs and in helping to identify their subject matter. Special thanks must go to David Bigger for sharing with me his vast knowledge of Derry's history and allowing me to use some of his many photographs. I am also grateful to Professor Richard McGowan and Terry Curran for their help and for granting permission to use prints from the photographic archives collection, University of Ulster, Magee College.

I am grateful to the Sisters of Mercy, Thornhill; Mr and Mrs Patrick Cooke; Mrs Hester Shearer; the Londonderry Port and Harbour Commissioners and Mr Gordon Wilson; the Derry City Council where Brian Lacey and Daniel Mugan were helpful; and St Columb's College and the staff of the library. All these people and institutions were helpful in giving permission for their photographs to be used.

Thanks are due to the Trustees of the Ulster Museum for granting permission to use photographs from the Welch Collection and the Hogg Collection; the trustees of the Ulster Folk and Transport Museum for the use of the Green photographs; and the National Library of Ireland for giving permission to use the Lawrence Collection. Only a selection of the many photographs held in the major public collections could be reproduced in a book of this size.

Finally, a word of thanks to my colleague Michael McLaughlin without whose work this book would have been impossible.

THE SETTING

This rather unusual view of the city centre, and its roofs, was taken from the spire of St Columb's Cathedral c. 1890. Both the old townhall — Corporation Hall — in the Diamond and the new townhall, without a clock in the tower — the Guildhall — at Shipquay Place can be seen. The sweep of the Foyle, the wooded demesne of St Columb's House (later to become St Columb's Park) in the Waterside and the masts of sailing ships are very visible. (Lawrence R2883)

This pre-1900 photograph looking across Carlisle Bridge towards the city shows densely packed housing stepping up the hillside and surmounted by the spire of St Columb's Cathedral. Three of Derry's shirt factories, Tillie and Henderson, R. Sinclair & Co. and Welch Margetson are easily identified by their sheer size. The turret of the jail can be seen against the skyline. The Great Northern Railway terminus by Carlisle Bridge was replaced by a new structure in 1899. The chimney stack in the Waterside belongs to Ballantine's steam corn mill. (Welch W07/22/1)

This view, dated 1863, predates the expansion of the Waterside up the hillside. It shows the old wooden bridge, made of oak and opened in 1790, with a turning mechanism to let ships sail upstream to Strabane. This toll bridge was shortly to be demolished, as Carlisle Bridge was already in place 200 yards upstream. Chapel Road Roman Catholic Church (St Columb's) can be seen standing in a green field site. Farm land is clearly visible. The chapel was built in 1841 on ground purchased in 1838 from Sir Robert Ferguson. The parochial hall and the distinctive gable and tower of Waterside Presbyterian Church were yet to be built. To the right of the bridge the main road to Dungiven in the 18th century — Fountain Hill — can be seen steeply climbing straight up the hill. The main road to Strabane joined Fountain Hill on the brow of the hill. Spencer Road had just been cut through at the Waterside to connect with Carlisle Bridge. The main street, previously known as Waterside, was renamed Duke Street. (Magee A182)

4

This photograph shows very clearly the growth of the Waterside up the hillside, c. 1900. (Lawrence C5379)

STREET SCENES

At the turn of the century a visitor would have entered the city along Carlisle Bridge which was built of steel and opened in 1863. It was a toll bridge with a draw bridge, opened by the centre section swinging on a very large pivot. This view along the bridge at ground level shows many pedestrians, all dressed in Edwardian finery. (Lawrence R2203)

Foyle Street. Once over the bridge there were two major thoroughfares to choose from — Foyle Street or Carlisle Road. The businessman would probably have chosen Foyle Street which was lined with warehouses, factories and mills. This view is looking along Foyle Street to the Guildhall c. 1900. Tram lines can be seen on the road. From 1897 to 1916 the horse drawn tram cars of the City of Derry Tramways Company ran from the Londonderry and Lough Swilly Railway terminus at Pennyburn, through Strand Road, Waterloo Place and Foyle Street to Carlisle Bridge. The City and Provincial Hotels and the coal merchants of Macdevette and Donnell are on the right and the offices of the Canadian Pacific Railway to the left, soon to be converted into the Criterion Hotel. (Lawrence R2548)

Carlisle Road would have given our visitor access to the historic heart of the city. This view is looking down Carlisle Road from Ferryquay Gate. To the right is the curved facade of the premises of Barr & McClements, merchant tailors, established in 1899 and to the left J. H. Dunlop & Son, which later became the Labour Exchange. The shirt factory of Welch Margetson is clearly visible. (Lawrence R246)

Ferryquay Gate gave entry to the 17th century walled city. The gate had been rebuilt in 1865 with a semi-circular arch for road traffic and round headed passages on either side of the arch for pedestrians. Through the gate can be seen the Anchor Bar, owned by A. A. Watt & Co., the Abbey Street distillers. Standing behind the causeway, very useful for pedestrians on those days when rain turned the road to mud, are young children, two of whom have bare feet. (Green WAG 977)

9

The Diamond. From Ferryquay Gate, Ferryquay Street led to the Diamond. This photograph was taken c. 1912. In 1910 Corporation Hall was demolished and the Diamond was laid out as a garden. The ''Black Man,'' the bronze statue of Sir Robert Ferguson, M.P. for the city from 1830 to 1860, standing at the top of Shipquay Street, was moved to Brooke Park in 1927 when the War Memorial was constructed at the Diamond. On the corner of Ferryquay Street can be seen the impressive premises of Austin's Department Store, rebuilt in 1906, and finished with a tower and copper-covered cupola. Its windows are filled from top to bottom with garments. On the other corner of Ferryquay Street stood Austin's Medical Hall. Next door, are Pickett & Co., jewellers since 1904 and beside it the shop of S. E. Caldwell, watch and clockmakers from 1905, with the Lending Library above. (Green WAG 997)

Butcher Gate. In addition to Ferryquay Street three other streets radiated from the Diamond — Butcher Street, Bishop Street and Shipquay Street. Through Butcher Gate from Butcher Street, can be seen two terrace houses, which are second-hand clothes shops with many clothes hanging on racks outside and piles of shoes beneath. To the right of the gate can be seen the public house of John McMonagle, on the corner with Magazine Street — his cellar doors are open, awaiting a delivery. There were iron rings above the grates on both sides of the street and ropes could be passed through these to lower barrels into the cellars. A constable of the R.I.C. is standing on top of the gate. The poster on the wall reads ''Aliens Restriction Order in Council.'' (Green WAG 992)

Bishop Street. Looking down Bishop Street from Bishop's Gate, Corporation Hall can be seen in the Diamond. The street is packed with people for a Relief of Derry (12 August) celebration. Sashes, banners, a Union Jack and people in procession can be seen at the bottom of the street. (Lawrence R3364)

MEMORIAL HALL. WALKER'S PILLAR. 2558. W.L.

Nailor's Row. Butcher Gate provided access to both Nailor's Row and the Bogside. Built under the shadow of the walls and starting at Butcher Gate this view shows nicely the character of Nailor's Row. The old lady standing on the street is overshadowed by the wall on one side and houses on the other. The street is further framed by the Apprentice Boy's Hall, Walker's monument and the grounds of St Augustine's Church of Ireland Chapel of Ease. (Lawrence R2558)

Shipquay Street was the fourth and final street leading from the
Diamond. Looking up Shipquay Street from Shipquay Gate,
Corporation Hall can be seen in the Diamond. When this photograph
was taken, c. 1880, the street was still lit by gas lamps. Electric light
replaced gas in 1894. The Georgian character of the street is very
evident. (Welch W07/17/12)

This is the same view of Shipquay Street as seen on the previous page but photographed at a later date, c. 1914. There is now no Corporation Hall in the Diamond. A ''Picture Palace'' has opened; in 1912 the Irish Motion Picture Company acquired the wholesale grocery premises of R. J. Black and opened Derry's first cinema. Beside the cinema the music shop of Henry B. Phillips, in business since 1903 and the offices of the Derry Standard, opened here in 1902, can be found. Across the street Edmiston & Co. have set up in new premises, built in 1902, beside the Belfast Bank. Halfway up Shipquay Street the Provincial Bank (built in 1890) and the Hibernian Bank (opened in 1896) are operating. The street is now lined with trees and lit by electricity. (Welch W07/17/11)

Bogside. This is a very interesting view, taken from the spire of St Columb's Cathedral, across the Bogside. It shows the Watt's distillery complex, including its distinctive buildings and chimneys. It further shows St Eugene's Cathedral with a square tower; the spire was begun in 1900 and completed in 1903. (Lawrence C5377)

*Shipquay Place. Through Shipquay Gate, Shipquay Street opened into
Shipquay Place. This was a busy junction as Foyle Street, Strand
Road and Shipquay Street met here. Jaunting cars and their drivers
waited for fares here, and horse drawn tram cars passed in both
directions. To the left are the walls and to the right the premises of
the Northern Bank, constructed in 1866 and the Northern Counties
Hotel, built in 1898. (Lawrence R2561)*

It was in Shipquay Place that the new townhall was built. This photograph, dated c. 1880 shows a rather shabby Shipquay Place with a coffee stand and a wooden hoarding on the site for the building of the Guildhall. Coffee stands (there were about six in all through the city) were erected by a local Temperance Society in order to discourage the drinking of alcohol. Rather dilapidated terrace buildings stand on the sites of what were to become the City Hotel and the lovely terrace block of 1-5 Shipquay Place. Stone causeways cross the road which looks very churned up and muddy. (Magee C783)

The laying of the foundation stone of the Guildhall in 1887. Foyle Street lies behind. One of the dilapidated terrace buildings at the junction with Foyle Street has been replaced, in 1882, by the rather grand terrace block of 1-5 Shipquay Place. People can be seen watching the ceremony from its roof. The building with the flag flying from its roof, beside the sculptured figure of Britannia, is Commercial Buildings, built in 1883 by William Mitchell, a flour and grain merchant, who formed his own shipping company, the Foyle Line, in 1890. (Derry City Council)

The construction of the Guildhall began c. 1888. The Harbour Commissioners' Office with its clock tower stands behind. The empty site beside the Harbour Office was filled by the premises of the Commercial Paper Company in 1892. (Derry City Council)

Compare this view with that of Shipquay Place in 1880 (page 18). The grand Guildhall stands on the site of the coffee stand, while at the junction of Foyle Street the City Hotel, built in 1888, and the block of 1-5 Shipquay Place, have replaced the two rather run-down buildings which were there in 1880. Shipquay Place was now a rather elegant place to view during a stroll along the city walls. (Hogg H07/17/20)

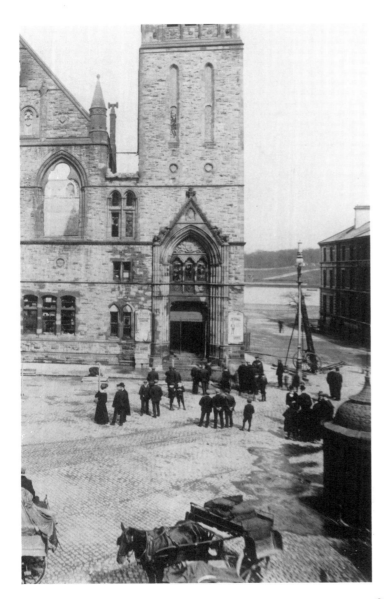

On Easter Sunday 1908 the Guildhall was badly damaged in a fire. Only the shell remained. This view was taken shortly after the fire. The fire brigade's turntable ladder still stands on the right, and crowds are gathered to gaze at the damage while clearing up is going on. Tram lines can be seen on the cobbled street. (Magee B563)

This view, c. 1913, shows the rebuilt Guildhall, which retained its basic outline with more elaborate window tracery. In the foreground is a small ironwork structure of eastern appearance. This was a public toilet, known locally as the ''iron man.'' (Welch W07/17/14)

*Adjoining Shipquay Place was Waterloo Place. By the ''Five Lamps''
drinking fountain, horses and carts gathered in front of the Ulster
Bank, built in 1858. Above the horse drawn tram car can be seen the
golden teapot, the symbol of W. J. McCullough, tea specialists and
high class grocers. (Lawrence R2898)*

Strand Road. Beyond Waterloo Place lay Strand Road, a major retail centre at the turn of the century. This print shows a cobbled street full of people c. 1912. On the right are Madden's tobacconists, established in 1904 and Glendennings Medical Hall, in operation from 1899 and makers of a perfume called the "Londonderry Air." The archway beside Glendenning's led to the offices and timber yard of R. Keys & Co. Beside this was G. F. Crook, which opened c. 1906, as a "Ladies and Mens Outfitters," with its window displaying tiers of hats and shirts. Next door was Victoria Police Barracks and beyond the police station stretched the market buildings which fronted Victoria Market. Access to the market from Strand Road was by way of an arched entrance. (Green WAG 991)

Aberfoyle Terrace. Derry was booming and new suburbs were springing up. This print is of a very neat and prim row of terrace houses, built in 1902, on the Strand Road and known as Aberfoyle Terrace. The road outside is cobbled and the terrace is bounded to the left by the trees of the Aberfoyle estate. (Hogg H07/17/15)

Crawford Square. This is another area where the well-to-do merchants of Derry lived. This terrace of three storey rendered buildings was completed around 1870. It was laid out around a grass square which was still immature when this photograph was taken. In the distance Ebrington Barracks in the Waterside, the clock tower of the Asylum, and the masts of sailing ships are clearly visible. (Lawrence R2881)

THE QUAY

The quay. This view from Corrody Hill in the Waterside shows the sweep of the River Foyle, the length of Derry's quays and the chimneys of the numerous steam mills along the river front on both sides of the Foyle. A large sailing vessel is docked near Carlisle Bridge, c. 1900. (Lawrence R1055)

Harbour Square on the quayside of Queen's quay in 1883. From 1869 to 1888 the Londonderry and Lough Swilly Railway Company ran trains over the Harbour Commissioners' lines to a terminal constructed here. A train is waiting to depart. Open cattle pens can be seen by the rail platform. During the livestock season over one thousand cattle were shipped weekly from Derry to Glasgow and Liverpool. The clock tower belongs to the Harbour Commissioners' Office which was built in 1882. The Guildhall had not yet been built in open ground behind the Harbour Office. Harbour Square was also the landing place for people using the ferries which crossed the Foyle. (Magee D509)

The quay formed the very heart of the city. Right up to the year 1902, and the end of the Foyle Line, sailing ships belonging to Derry merchants could be seen tied up along the quay. This photograph dated 1881 and titled ''Minnehaha and other Derry owned ships'' shows Queen's quay bursting with sailing vessels. The Minnehaha was for thirty five years under the house flag of William McCorkell & Co. In 1881 William McCorkell & Co. had a fleet of eight ships constantly employed in the Baltimore grain run. These sailing ships were all barque rigged which meant they could be run economically with a small crew and they usually made three round trip trans-atlantic voyages per year. The import of Baltimore grain into Derry was at its peak in 1881 when the McCorkell fleet brought in some 20,000 tons of grain. The ships can be seen here tied up outside McCorkell's massive five storey high grain mill. (Magee A127)

This view of Queen's quay was taken at the turn of the century. The Guildhall can be seen in the background. Steamers are tied up along the quay. The Glasgow steamers by the 1880s carried 3,500 passengers annually from Derry, many of them seasonal harvesters.

Freight carriages await loading on the track built by the Harbour Commissioners to connect boat with train. The large five storey building is McCorkell's grain mill. In 1916 they built a new mill behind this one. (Lawrence R2563)

This photograph taken c. 1900 shows the footbridge which took people over the railway line to the ferry at Ebrington Barracks, which crossed to Harbour Square. Six large sailing ships are docked at Queen's quay. (Lawrence R2876)

The landing stage at Harbour Square on Queen's quay for the ferries which crossed the Foyle from Ebrington Barracks and the Northern Counties Railway terminus in the Waterside. Three small steam launches, the Roe, Foyle and S.M. Alexander ran a ferry service, every ten minutes, between here and the Waterside in the decade before the First World War. It is the S.M. Alexander which is seen here tied up at the landing stage. St Columb's Roman Catholic Church, the Reformed Presbyterian Church and Waterside Presbyterian Church stand out very clearly in the Waterside. The railway terminus and carriages of the Northern Counties Railway can also be seen. (Lawrence R2892)

This view across the Foyle from Garrison ferry at Ebrington Barracks shows two steamers along the quayside. It shows both the Guildhall and Corporation Hall and any view of both these buildings together must predate 1908. (Lawrence R2879)

The iron paddle steamer, Albatross, seen here moored at the quay, operated a ferry service between Derry and Moville during the years 1878 to 1906. From the early 1860s right through to 1939 transatlantic passenger steamers anchored at Moville, in the deeper water of Lough Foyle, some 18 miles downstream from Derry to take emigrants to Canada and the U.S.A. Passengers were carried, free of charge, from Derry's quay to Moville on tenders such as the Albatross. During the summer the Albatross would have been a pleasure cruiser. (Magee B157)

The paddle steamer Samson seen here, was a tug which operated on Lough Foyle during the 1870s and 1880s. At peak times the Samson offered pleasure cruises on the Foyle. In the distance, set amongst a wooded demesne is the ''Farm'' which was, at one time, the residence of Sir Robert Alexander Ferguson, M.P. for the city from 1830 to 1860. (Lawrence R2890)

The crew of the S.S. Laurentic being entertained at the Guildhall on 1st February 1917. A banquet was held in their honour by the Mayor, Sir Robert Anderson, who can be seen standing at the head of the centre table. On 25th January 1917 the S.S. Laurentic, a White Star liner converted to an auxiliary cruiser, under the command of Captain Reginald Norton, with a crew of 12 officers and 1,047 men, sailing for Halifax, Nova Scotia, with 43 tonnes of gold and silver on board, pulled into port at the Royal Navy base at Buncrana. The ship only stayed a few hours to discharge a small number of ratings before resuming its journey. On leaving Lough Swilly the ship was either torpedoed by a German U-Boat or hit by a mine off Fanad Head. In any case the Laurentic sank with the loss of 354 lives including that of local man, Lieutenant Steel from Ivy Terrace. Most of the gold was eventually recovered. (Magee C696)

BUILDINGS AND SHOPS

St Columb's Cathedral. This lovely picture of St Columb's Cathedral was taken c. 1900 from the top of Pump Street. An old lady stands in the right foreground while a group, including one boy without shoes, are standing or sitting inside the gate. St Columb's was built between 1628 and 1633 to serve as the parish church, as well as a cathedral. (Welch W07/17/15)

St Eugene's Cathedral. The foundation stone for the Roman Catholic cathedral was laid in 1851 but it was 1873 before it was completed. It was built in the grounds of the Dominican priory which was founded by O'Donnell, chief of Tyrconnel in 1274. The spire was added in 1903. (Lawrence R2880)

First Derry Presbyterian Church. This view predates 1903, as the porticos have not yet been built. This photograph may have been taken after the restoration work of 1896. There has been a Presbyterian Church on this site since 1690. The main body of this particular building dates from 1780. (Lawrence R2886)

First Derry Presbyterian Church. This view postdates 1903 as the porticos of red sandstone were built at that time. (Hogg H07/17/9)

Foyle College. This well proportioned Georgian building was constructed in 1814 at Lawrence Hill on ground which was then outside the city. It replaced the former Free Diocesan School in Society Street founded in 1617. In 1868 Londonderry Academical Institution was established by local merchants on East Wall. In 1871 the school moved to a new building, known as the Academy, on Academy Road. In 1896 it amalgamated with Foyle College, with the Academy becoming the boarding house for pupils attending school at Lawrence Hill. (Lawrence R2565)

St Columb's College. On Monday 3rd November 1879 St Columkille's College, funded largely by the Bishop and clergy of the Diocese of Derry, opened its doors for day pupils and boarders to prepare them "for Maynooth and other Ecclesiastical Colleges; also for the Civil Service Examinations, and for the Intermediate Examinations," as detailed in an advertisement in the Londonderry Journal, 20 October 1879. The College was built in the grounds of Frederick Hervey, the fourth Earl of Bristol and the Bishop of Derry from 1768 to 1803. The school incorporated the Casino built by Hervey which was modelled on villas he had seen in Italy during a tour of the Continent. (Lawrence R2903)

Gwyn's Institute. John Gwyn, who came from Muff, County Donegal, to start a grocery business on Bishop Street, left on his death in 1829, £40,000 for the education and upkeep of orphan boys. Gwyn's Institute was erected for this purpose in 1840 on ten acres of land purchased for £200. During the cholera epidemic of 1832 there were so many destitute children that a hotel was rented in Shipquay Street to house them until the Institute was opened. In 1901 the building became a museum. (Lawrence R2210)

Orphans on the steps of Gwyn's Institute c. 1890. (David Bigger)

Corporation Hall. The first townhall was erected in the Diamond in 1616. It was destroyed during the siege of 1689 and replaced in 1692 by another building in which the assembly rooms were located above an open arcaded market where grain and potatoes were sold. It was demolished in 1823 and replaced by the Corporation Hall, with its main curved entrance facing Bishop Street. It served as the townhall until 1890 when the Guildhall opened at Shipquay Place. Corporation Hall was demolished in 1910. The Diamond was then laid out as a garden. (Lawrence R1227)

Graham's Warehouse. This lovely picture was taken around 1900 of the shop and impressive looking window display of William Graham & Co., music sellers and pianoforte tuners and dealers. They even supplied bands for evening parties. LONDON PIANOFORTE WAREHOUSE in large letters identified the extensive premises of this *business at the Diamond, between Baldrick & Co. (on the corner with Bishop Street) and George Austin & Co. (on the corner with Ferryquay Street). In 1905 William Graham & Co. moved to new premises in the Market Buildings on Strand Road. (Lawrence R6202)*

This photograph, taken in 1906, is of the shop front of Robert Elder's grocery business at 21 Duke Street in the Waterside. The firm also sold hardware, artificial manures and agricultural seeds. This may be the owner himself standing outside the shop with his employees. (Magee B147)

This picture taken about 1905 outside R. R. A. Floyd's music shop
in Pump Street, seems to be part of a promotion to increase
gramophone sales. A gramophone can be seen on the bonnet of the
Daimler car. The rather stern looking owner, R. R. A. Floyd, is
standing at the doorway to the shop. (David Bigger)

THE BIG HOUSE

The Big House symbolised the status of the local gentry and the successful rise of local businessmen who still dominated social life at the turn of the century.

St Columb's House. Set amongst a wooded, undulating demesne the large two storey stuccoed house of St Columb's in the Waterside was home, for a period, for the Cooke family. The grounds of this house now form St Columb's Park. In 1837 John and Joseph Cooke began a partnership that lasted until John Cooke's death on 25th February 1895. In the period 1839 to 1868 this family partnership bought twelve ships for the North American emigrant and timber trade. J. & J. Cooke forged very close links between Derry and the eastern maritime provinces of Canada.

In this view can be seen Joseph Cooke, co-founder of J. & J. Cooke, with his six children outside St Columb's House on 24th October 1895. Standing at the back (from the left) are Thomas Fitzpatrick Cooke who married Aileen Babington in 1908 and lived at Caw House in the Waterside, Frances Cooke who married George Gilliland of Brookhall, Joseph Cooke who died on 19 June 1896 and Archie Cooke who lived at Government House on the Letterkenny Road. Seated in the front (from the left) are Harry Cooke who lived at Boom Hall, John F. Cooke, a barrister, and Joseph Cooke. (Mr and Mrs Patrick Cooke)

In this view at Boom Hall, c. 1890, Joseph Cooke and his wife Frances can be seen seated by the entrance porch. George Gilliland, smoking a pipe, is standing holding the reins of his horse; beside him is his wife, Frances Cooke. The Gillilands lived at Brookhall which was built c. 1790 for George Fitzgerald Hill, M.P. for the city, who identified Wolfe Tone on his landing at Buncrana after the ill-fated attempt by the French Fleet to enter Lough Swilly in October 1798 to support the United Irishmen's rebellion. In 1839 Brookhall was bought by Henry Barre Beresford before passing to the Gilliland family in 1856. George and Frances Gilliland's youngest son, Valentine, a captain in the Royal Irish Rifles, was killed in action at Ypres on 7th May 1915. Archie Cooke is seated on horseback while two of his brothers, John, wearing the fez, and Harry, are leaning against the wall. (Mr and Mrs Patrick Cooke)

Thornhill. This house was built in 1882-85 for Andrew Alexander Watt, the High Sheriff of County Londonderry, on an impressive site overlooking the Foyle. The Watt family had first come to Derry from Ramelton in 1762 and established the business of Andrew A. Watt & Co. in Bishop Street. In 1839 the Watt's acquired full ownership of the Abbey Street distillery which by 1880 was the largest in Ireland. This rapid growth was reflected in their share of distributed profits, which amounted to over £10,000 annually, by 1880. Andrew A. Watt who had married Violet Flora De Burgh of Millbank House, County Kildare, on 7th October 1875 could, therefore, afford to build a large baronial house. In this view four members of the Watt family (from left) Sam, Gerald, Constance and Eva, are seated on horseback outside the house, c. 1890. (Sisters of Mercy, Thornhill)

The Drawing Room, Thornhill. The ornate and cluttered look of a wealthy Victorian household is very evident in this interior view of Thornhill. From 1932 Thornhill has been the home of Thornhill College which must have one of the most impressive sites of any school in Ireland. (Sisters of Mercy, Thornhill)

In the late 19th century and early 20th century the most exclusive club in Derry would have been the Derry Harriers which included most of Derry's moneyed and propertied families. In 1888 the Harriers in all their riding finery were captured on photograph at Thornhill. Third from the right in the back row is David Watt. Tom F. Cooke stands second from left in the front row and to his right are Violet Watt, the wife of Andrew Alexander Watt, and his brother John F. Cooke. George Gilliland of Brookhall is standing in the centre, holding a riding crop, with Archie Cooke, Dudley McCorkell and Andrew Alexander Watt, master of the Derry Hunt, to his left. (Mr and Mrs Patrick Cooke)

In this view the Derry Hunt is gathering at Caw House in the Waterside, c. 1912. Thomas Fitzpatrick Cooke bought Caw in 1909 from the Alexander family. Tom was master of the Derry Hunt and he is seen here, seated on a white horse, with the pack of hounds around him. Seated on the dark horse is his brother Archie Cooke. In a notice of meetings to be held in February 1913, members of the Derry Harriers were advised, ''Gentlemen riding with these hounds are most particularly requested to carefully avoid turnips and newly laid down grass and clover.'' The Harriers also organised point-to-point races at Ballyarnet. (Mr and Mrs Patrick Cooke)

Boom Hall was the setting for many social gatherings. On 9th August 1898 a garden party was held here to welcome the annual visit of the Irish Society. Many of the city's dignitaries were received by their hosts the Mayor, Sir John B. Johnston and his wife. The three men standing at the very back, looking slightly out of place, are employees of Sir John. David Cleghorn Hogg, who in 1898 with his partner Charles Mitchell, opened the five storeyed shirt factory on Great James Street is seated with hat in hand (ninth from the left). David Hogg, born in Melrose, Scotland and married to Jane Cooke of Ramelton, County Donegal, was Vice President of the Londonderry Liberal Association. He was to cause consternation among Unionist ranks by being elected Liberal M.P. for the city in 1913. (David Bigger)

Dated November 28th 1886, and titled ''Britannia,'' Violet Flora Watt (née De Burgh), the wife of Andrew Alexander Watt of Thornhill, displays the regal outfit she wore on her presentation to the court of Queen Victoria. (Mr and Mrs Patrick Cooke)

OCCASIONS

A fascinating view of the 12th August parade of 1865 along the city walls above Ferryquay Gate. Stallholders have set up on the street by the gate. This photograph shows Ferryquay Gate in its original form. It was this gate that the Apprentice Boys of Derry closed in the face of James II's troops in 1688. (Magee A195)

The laying of the foundation stone of the senior house of St Columb's College, Bishop Street, on 30 June 1892 with the Catholic bishop, John Keys O'Doherty, officiating. The other priests in attendance, subsequently became bishops of Derry in their turn; Charles McHugh (1907–26) and Bernard O'Kane (1926–39).

On 28th July 1903, King Edward VII, Queen Alexandra and Princess Victoria arrived at Harbour Square on the royal steam locomotive, aptly named "Edward VII." The party had arrived at Buncrana on board HMS Victoria and Albert. The Derry Journal gave details of the day's events. On arrival the royal party was driven by carriage up Shipquay Street to the Diamond where Corporation Hall was decorated as a medieval castle for the visit. (Magee D351)

From the Diamond, the royal carriage left by Ferryquay Street. Here the royal entourage can be seen moving down Carlisle Road, which is festooned with flags, in glorious sunshine. Edward VII is in the front carriage, saluting the crowd of people and military guard of honour which line both sides of the street as far as the eye can see. To the right, people can be seen hanging their heads out of the windows of the Opera House. Beyond the Opera House, scaffolding encases the spire of the newly erected Methodist church. The party returned by John Street and Foyle Street to the Guildhall where the King lunched with the Mayor, Alderman Marshall Tillie. After lunch the royal party went to the borough infirmary at the top of Clarendon Street. At 3 p.m. they visited Brooke Park where they planted oak saplings. The King then presented the South Africa war medals to the officers of the First Battalion Inniskilling Fusiliers. The party returned by Clarendon Street and at 4 p.m. left the city by train for Buncrana to board their ship, their next destination being Galway Bay. (Magee B154)

The choir pose for a picture with the Church of Ireland Bishop of Derry and Raphoe outside St Columb's Cathedral after the St Columb's day service in 1903. Bishop Chadwick is seated in front of the verger. (David Bigger)

The headmaster and senior pupils of St Columb's Hall school, c. 1910. St Columb's Hall was built in 1888 as a Temperance Hall. Its basement housed ''The Hall'' school which was established to educate the Catholic children of dockers who lived in the Orchard Street/Bridge Street area. The school later moved to purpose-built premises at the top of Bridge Street and became known as St Patrick's Boys School. (Magee A777)

By 1914 the prospect of violent conflict between two opposing Volunteer movements in Ulster loomed. Unionist resistance to the Third Home Rule Bill, to give Ireland a limited measure of independence within the Empire, saw the creation of citizen armies which in January 1913 were drawn together under one command — the Ulster Volunteer Force. By February 1914 the U.V.F. consisted of 100,000 men. In January 1915 ''B'' Company of the 2nd Battalion City of Derry Regiment U.V.F. was photographed by E. G. Harries who had a studio on Bishop Street. It shows four rows of men, wearing bandoliers and caps, with six boys sitting in front, each holding a rifle or gun. Pride of place seems to be taken by a mounted machine gun. They are lined up outside the building which was later to become the headquarters of the ''B'' Specials on Hawkins Street. (David Bigger)

Meanwhile the Irish Volunteers were formed at a great meeting in the Rotunda in Dublin on 25th November 1913, with the purpose of ensuring the implementation of Home Rule. Membership of the Irish Volunteers grew rapidly to 180,000 men in 1914. In this picture, c. 1914, men of the Irish Volunteers are gathering to drill at Celtic Park Recreation Grounds off the Lone Moor Road. One man is dressed in uniform with a ceremonial sword hanging from his belt. (Magee C741)

With the outbreak of the First World War in 1914, people's energies were, in many cases, now directed towards the war effort. In this view crowds are gathered in front of the Guildhall and the City Hotel in 1916 to hand over an ambulance, donated by the people of Derry.

Standing at the entrance to the Guildhall, wearing his robes, is the Mayor, Robert Newton Anderson, who lived at Deanfield House in the Waterside. (Magee B015)

The Mayor, Robert Newton Anderson, is seen here visiting the
Londonderry War Hospital Supply Depot on the Asylum Road in
1914. Five nurses and one army officer are standing with the Mayor.
(Magee B016)

AT WORK

The shirt industry was Derry's major employer and the profitability of this industry, at the turn of the century, was reflected not only in the size of shirt factories but in their architectural grandeur. In 1864, McIntyre, Hogg, Marsh & Co. moved to large and modern premises at the City Factory in Queen Street. This picture taken in 1905 shows the vast size of the factory, and the decorative brick work. (Hogg H07/17/10)

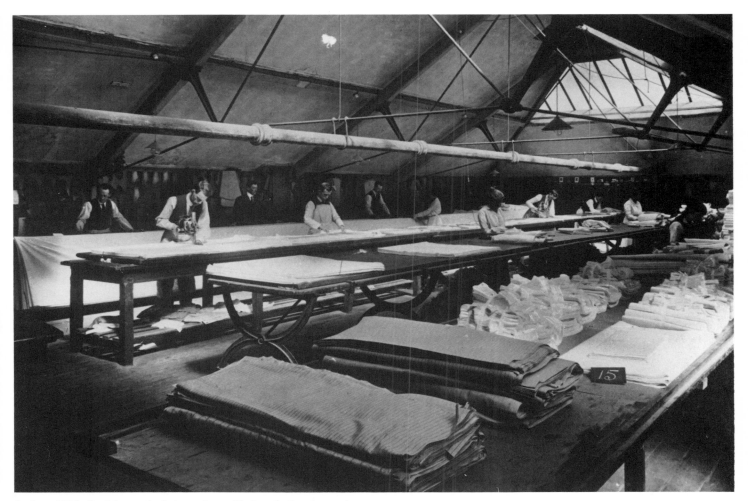

*In June 1919, the Liverpool photographers, Sir Joseph Causton and
Sons, were commissioned to photograph the various shirt making
operations within the City Factory. Here men can be seen cutting the
cloth in the shirt cutting room. This was the only operation in which
men were involved in the production of shirts. Most workers in the
shirt industry were women. (Magee C078)*

This photograph shows the collar machine room, with row upon row of girls working their steam powered sewing machines. (Magee C072)

The collar laundry department of the City Shirt Factory, June 1919.
(Magee C074)

Watt's distillery at Abbey Street was a major male employer in the city. Men can be seen here packing and labelling "The Tyrconnel Whiskey," c. 1912. (Magee B295)

When Watt's distillery closed in 1921 the trades of coopering, carting and blacksmithing suffered. In 1887 50,000 casks of whiskey were stored in Watt's bonded warehouses. Watt's furthermore, had maintained a large fleet of horse drawn carts for their transport needs. Here flat carts can be seen outside the distillery's warehouse, with barrels and cartons on board, c. 1912. (Magee B298)

The launch of the S.S. New York News *from the North of Ireland Shipbuilding Company yard at Pennyburn on Wednesday 24th May 1922. The 2,300 ton* S.S. New York News *was built for the Ontario Paper Company, which was owned by Colonel McCormick, proprietor of the* Chicago Tribune, *to ply the Canadian lakes carrying wood pulp. The lady standing on the platform with a bunch of flowers in her hand is Irene Rogers, who launched the ship. She was the daughter of H. M. Rogers who supervised the ship's construction. (Harbour Commissioners)*

Outside the offices of the North of Ireland Shipbuilding Company, the guests invited to the launch of the Ville D'Arras *in September 1917 were photographed. Many of the guests in the line up are French as the ship was built for a French Company. The town clerk, Sir Henry Miller, is standing in the back row (third from the left). (Harbour Commissioners)*

This print is of the three buses of Roberts & Sons outside the back of the Guildhall in 1913. The bus on the right, with 32 seats, operated on the Derry-Claudy-Feeny route and went into service in August 1912. Another bus ran on the Derry-Moville-Greencastle route which was the company's first service. In 1913 the company began a night mail service to Strabane, Letterkenny, Milford and Portsalon. During the First World War they operated a bus to Limavady which was powered by town gas. Standing in front of the buses are the owners, Hugh Roberts, Reginald Roberts and Charles Roberts. At this time Roberts & Sons were the only public service operator in the North West. (Magee B086)

John Brewster operated the Model Bakery from premises on Little James Street. This view is of three Brewster's bakery delivery vans in 1904, waiting in Great James Street. (Magee B150)

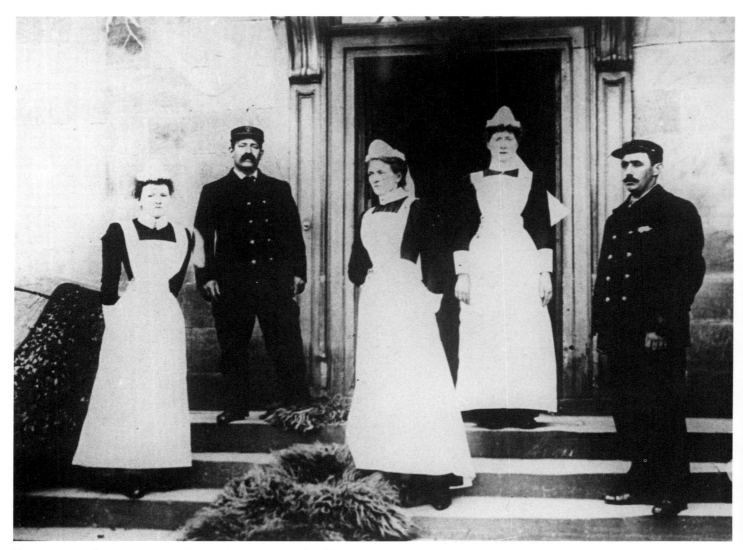

Three nurses and two porters standing at the entrance to the old lunatic asylum. (Magee D661)

The engine room staff of the S.S. Cedar in 1885. The S.S. Cedar operated on the Derry-Glasgow route from 1878 to 1906. It often partnered the Azalea on the Portrush-Glasgow daylight service. The crew have some of their engine room implements with them, including an oil can. The man seated in the middle seems to be holding a valve. (David Bigger)

A deputation from the city council is seen here at Cabry in the Inishowen peninsula, County Donegal, in August 1881, examining one possible source for increasing the water supply to the city. Richard Hassard, the consulting engineer (second from left along the back row), recommended the Cabry supply but the shirt manufacturers of Derry vetoed it. In the foreground (from left) are included Henry Darcus, Sir Edward Reid — the Mayor, Sir Robert McVicker and Sir William Miller. Councillors and engineers made up the remainder of the party. The problem of obtaining a good water supply remained for many years. (Derry City Council)

The Board of Directors of the Londonderry Gaslight Company in 1877. Seated clockwise: James Thompson; Robert Newton, Director of the Letterkenny Railway; Bartholomew McCorkell, Director of William McCorkell & Co.; William McCarter, Chairman; Joseph Cooke, Director of J. & J. Cooke; James Corscaden; and James Allan. Standing is the manager Mr McNee. It was a tradition that the manager and engineers of the Gaslight Company were Scottish. Gaslight was introduced to Derry in 1829; the gateway to the original gasyard still stands on Foyle Street. Electric light replaced gas light on the principal streets of the city in 1894. (Mrs Shearer)

AT LEISURE

The cast of a theatre company, standing on stage at the Opera House, c. 1880. In 1876 a theatre opened at the Opera House on Carlisle Road. The previous theatre, which had opened in 1789 at the junction of Artillery Lane and London Street, was closed by 1830. It had relied too much on the patronage of the gentry and officers of the garrison who tended to support the theatre on the big social occasions associated with the summer assizes and the Londonderry Races. The Opera House, with its elegant interior, offered a greater variety of entertainment. Travelling opera, theatre and musical companies visited the city, with pantomimes at Christmas being the biggest draw. For its last ten years the Opera House, which was burnt down in 1939, only showed films. (Magee C700)

"Thompson in Tir na nÓg." Amateur theatricals at St Columb's
College, 1915. *(St Columb's College)*

The Londonderry Young People's band, 1917. Seated in the front row are two members of the Salvation Army. This picture was taken in the Salvation Army Hall on Carlisle Road. (Magee C583)

In addition to the theatre and music, sport was an important leisure pursuit. This early print shows polo players and horses at the polo pitch at Gransha. One gentleman has a very distinctive beard. The players were mostly from the army garrison based at Ebrington barracks. In later years the polo pitch moved to Beechgrove. (Magee B149)

*A photograph of the Londonderry Academical Institution Lacrosse
team of 1883 in typical Victorian pose. The team members are either
standing, leaning, sitting or lying down in front of an entrance to the
Academy. (David Bigger)*

An athletic meeting at the Brandywell grounds c. 1910. In this picture two runners seem to be recovering after a hard race. The track is ringed by a crowd of spectators. (David Bigger)

SELECT BIBLIOGRAPHY AND FURTHER READING

Willie Carson, **Yesterday . . . when our troubles seemed so far away.** Derry, 1982.

Sholto Cooke, **The maiden city and the Western Ocean.** Dublin, N.D.

J B Doyle, **Tours in Ulster,** pp 280-306. Dublin 1854, Repr., Ballynahinch.

Charles Gallagher, **Acorns and oak leaves — A Derry childhood.** Derry.

Mr and Mrs S C Hall, **Ireland, its scenery, character etc.,** pp. 374-376. London 1841, Repr. London 1984, as **Hall's Ireland.**

Sam Hughes, **City on the Foyle.** Derry, 1984.

The industries of Ireland, Part 1 Belfast and the towns of the north, pp 147-156. London 1891, Repr. Belfast 1986, as **Industries of the north one hundred years ago.**

De Latocnaye, **A Frenchman's Walk through Ireland 1796-7,** pp 198-202. Cork, 1798, Repr. Belfast 1984.

Vera McFadden, **Island city.** Derry, 1982.

T H Mullan, **Ulster's historic city — Derry Londonderry.** Coleraine, 1986.

Ordnance Survey of Ireland, memoir of the city and liberties of Londonderry. Dublin 1837.

Robert Lloyd Praeger, **The way that I went,** pp 62-3. Dublin, 1937, Repr. Dublin, 1980.

Alistair Rowan, **The buildings of Ireland, North West Ulster.** London 1979.

Rev. George Vaughan Sampson, **Survey of County Londonderry.** London, 1814.

Robert Simpson, **The annals of Derry.** Londonderry 1847, Repr. Limavady, 1987.

William Makepeace Thackery, **The Irish sketch book,** pp 335-352. London 1843, Repr. Belfast 1985.

Ulster Architectural Heritage Society, **Historic buildings in and near the city of Derry.** Belfast 1970.